Perfect Guide to
Casting On & Binding Off

HOW TO BEGIN AND END YOUR KNITTING WITH CONFIDENCE

Jen Lucas

Landauer Publishing

PERFECT GUIDE TO CASTING ON & BINDING OFF

Landauer Publishing, www.landauerpub.com, is an imprint of Fox Chapel Publishing Company, Inc.

Copyright © 2025 by Jen Lucas and Fox Chapel Publishing Company, Inc.

All rights reserved. No part of this book may be reproduced, stored in a retrieval system, or transmitted in any form or by any means, electronic, mechanical, photocopying, recording, or otherwise, without the prior written permission of Fox Chapel Publishing, except for the inclusion of brief quotations in an acknowledged review and the enlargement of the template patterns in this book for personal use only. The patterns themselves, however, are not to be duplicated for resale or distribution under any circumstances. Any such copying is a violation of copyright law.

Project Team
Acquisitions Editor: Amelia Johanson
Editor: Jeremy Hauck
Copy Editor: Christa Oestreich
Designer: Mike Deppen
Proofreader & Indexer: Jean Bissell

Shutterstock used: legkost (front cover, main); NOVA STOCK 6 (yarn, 12–13, 24–27, 38–39, 48–51, 56–57, 60–61); Alla Koala (yarn ball, 64)

ISBN 978-1-63981-136-6

Library of Congress Control Number: 2025936616

To learn more about the other great books from Fox Chapel Publishing, or to find a retailer near you, call toll-free at 800-457-9112 or visit us at www.FoxChapelPublishing.com.
You can also send mail to:
Fox Chapel Publishing
903 Square Street
Mount Joy, PA 17552

We are always looking for talented authors.
To submit an idea, please send a brief inquiry to acquisitions@foxchapelpublishing.com.

Printed in China
First printing

This book has been published with the intent to provide accurate and authoritative information in regard to the subject matter within. While every precaution has been taken in the preparation of this book, the author and publisher expressly disclaim any responsibility for any errors, omissions, or adverse effects arising from the use or application of the information contained herein.

Contents

Introduction 5
Knitting Supplies 6
Getting Started 11
Cast Ons 17
Bind Offs...............41
Index................. 63
About the Author 64

Introduction

For many of us, when we begin our knitting journey, we learn a cast on and a bind off, and those are the ones we use exclusively on our first projects. However, it doesn't take long to realize that there's a whole cast-on and bind-off world out there waiting for us to explore!

There are so many ways that knitters have learned these essential techniques—whether through books, videos, or a face-to-face connection with a family member or friend. As a result, we sometimes see variations in these cast ons and bind offs. And that's okay! As long as we're getting our stitches on and off the needles, that's all that matters. The little differences in our stitches are what make the knitting community so wonderful, allowing us to connect and tell our stories with and through our knitting.

In the book, I show how to work the cast ons and bind offs using the English (or throwing) method of knitting, with the yarn in my right hand, and I am also right-handed. You can work all these techniques using your own style of knitting; you may need to adjust your hands and yarn slightly for it to feel comfortable for you. If you knit truly left-handed (i.e., the mirror image), then you will need to work all steps in this book as their mirror image.

I hope this book brings you lots of inspiration for your future projects!

—Jen *(she/her)*

Knitting Supplies

Knitting Needles

Knitting needles come in all shapes, sizes, and materials. Circular needles have various cable lengths.

Knitting needles are obviously one of the essential tools for this craft. The type of knitting needles you need depends on what project you're doing and your personal preferences. Needles are commonly made from aluminum or different types of wood but can also be made from a variety of other materials.

Another knitting needle consideration is needle length. You can use straight, circular, or double-pointed knitting needles (DPNs). These all come in different material types and length.

I find having some spare DPNs available for casting on and binding off to be useful. Sometimes you need an extra needle to help you with a tricky part, or you need one to complete a particular bind off like the three-needle bind off (page 56).

Knitting Needle Guide

Here's a quick reference for the most common knitting needle sizes.

US Size	Millimeters	US Size	Millimeters
0	2mm	9	5.5mm
1	2.25mm	10	6mm
1.5	2.5mm	10.5	6.5mm
2	2.75mm	11	8mm
2.5	3mm	13	9mm
3	3.25mm	15	10mm
4	3.5mm	17	12mm
5	3.75mm	19	15mm
6	4mm	35	19mm
7	4.5mm	50	25mm
8	5mm	70	35mm

Yarns

The yarn you choose is critical to the finished look of your project.

Besides the knitting needles, the other thing you absolutely need for your knitting project is the yarn. Yarn choice affects every aspect of the project, so it's important to take some time to think and plan for the yarn you'll be using. For the tutorial projects in this book, I used Swish Worsted and Wool of the Andes Worsted from KnitPicks.

One of the critical factors in your yarn choice is thickness. Yarn thickness is defined by the yarn weight, and there are industry standards that almost every yarn company uses. If you find a pattern that calls for a #4/worsted/medium yarn, that is the yarn weight you'll want to use for your project. Changing the weight of yarn you're using for a pattern greatly affects the gauge of the project. Gauge is the number of stitches and rows (or rounds) in a specified area, often 4" x 4" (10.2 x 10.2cm). Some knitters may be comfortable with changing the weight of the yarn for a specific pattern, which is amazing. Just know that, most of the time, this change comes with some calculating you'll have to do on your own.

Yarn Weight Guide

Here's a quick reference of the Standard Yarn Weight System from the Craft Yarn Council (CYC). Remember, this chart is just a guide—it's a starting point. If you're working from a specific pattern, follow the yarn weight and gauge information for that project.

Yarn Weight & Name	Type of Yarn	Gauge in Stockinette Stitch over 4" (10.2cm)	Recommended US Needle Size
LACE 0	Lace, 10-count crochet thread	33–40 sts*	000–1*
SUPER FINE 1	Sock, Fingering, Baby	27–32 sts	1–3
FINE 2	Sport, Baby	23–26 sts	3–5
LIGHT 3	DK, Light Worsted	21–24 sts	5–7
MEDIUM 4	Worsted, Afghan, Aran	16–20 sts	7–9
BULKY 5	Bulky, Chunky	12–15 sts	9–11
SUPER BULKY 6	Super Bulky, Roving	7–11 sts	11–17
JUMBO 7	Jumbo, Roving	6 sts or less	17 and larger

*Lace yarns are typically knit using larger needles to create loose, lacy patterns. Be sure to follow the recommendations for needle size and gauge included in your pattern.

Notions

What are notions? They are all the little tools that you need to complete your project, like stitch markers, scissors, tapestry needles, and so much more. As you continue your knitting journey, you'll find yourself adding more notions to your toolbox as needed.

For casting on or binding off a project, there are few notions that you might find especially useful. You may see patterns where stitch markers are added to the needle while casting on, or where a stitch marker is used to mark a stitch before binding off. There are some cast ons, like the Provisional Cast On (page 35), that call for a crochet hook or some bind offs that need that extra knitting needle, like a double-pointed needle. A tapestry needle or yarn needle, as well as scissors, is a necessity for finishing a bind off and completing your project. As a knitter, you'll figure out quickly which notions work best for you and your projects.

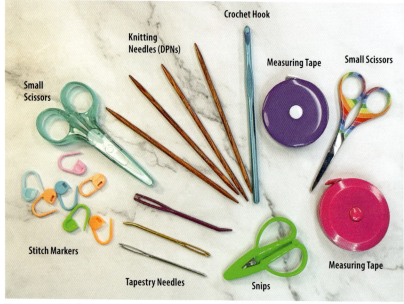

There are a number of tools you can use for cast-on and bind-off techniques or to measure a gauge swatch.

Getting Started

Most knitting patterns simply state to cast on a specific number of stitches to begin a project, and to bind off a specific number of stitches to finish it. There are dozens of cast ons and bind offs, so how do you know which one to actually use?

Choosing cast ons and bind offs. It's important to read a pattern all the way through before beginning so you can make some decisions about your cast on and bind off. Does the pattern start with ribbing? Then you might like an Alternating Long Tail Cast On (page 21) or a Tubular Cast On (page 38). Are you finishing a top-down shawl? Consider my personal favorite, the Knit Two Stitches Together Through the Back Loop Bind Off (page 44) or leave yourself some extra yarn and work a decorative I-Cord Bind Off (page 54). Some patterns will tell you specifically which cast on or bind off to use, but often it's up to the knitter to decide what's best for them.

The working yarn. Sometimes you'll see a cast-on or bind-off instruction tell you to use the "working yarn." This term refers to the yarn that you're currently working with—the strand that is going to your ball of yarn. You will see this most often in cast-on instructions where you're using both the yarn tail and the working yarn to add stitches to the knitting needle.

Abbreviations

Here are the common knitting abbreviations used throughout this book.

BO	bind off	k2tog	knit two stitches together
CO	cast on	p	purl
DPN(s)	double-pointed needle(s)	tbl	through the back loop
k	knit	tog	together

Basic Stitches

To cast on and bind off for a project, there are a few basic stitches you need to know.

Slip Knot

A slip knot is the first step for starting most knitting projects. There are lots of ways to make a slip knot—this is the method I like to use when teaching others about knitting basics. It's both easy to do and easy to learn.

1. Leaving a 4"–6" (10.2–15.2cm) yarn tail, create a loop with the yarn tail going over the working yarn.

2. Take the loop and fold it down over the working yarn. You will have something that looks a little like a pretzel.

3. You'll see three strands, with the center strand being the working yarn. Take a knitting needle and go over the bottom strand, under the middle strand, and over the top strand with it.

4. Pull on both the yarn tail and the working yarn to tighten the loop on the needle. Your slip knot is complete.

Knit Stitch

1. With the yarn in back (behind the work), insert the right needle into the front of the first stitch on the left needle, from left to right.

2. Wrap the yarn counterclockwise around the right needle.

3. Bring the yarn through the stitch on the left needle.

4. Remove the stitch from the left needle. The new stitch is on the right needle.

Purl Stitch

1. With the yarn in back (behind the work), insert the right needle into the front of the first stitch on the left needle, from right to left.

2. Wrap the yarn counterclockwise around the right needle.

3. With the yarn on the needle, bring the right needle back through the stitch from left to right.

4. Remove the stitch from the left needle. The new stitch is on the right needle.

Yarn Over

A yarn over can be worked several different ways, depending on a variety of factors as to why it's worked one way or the other. Most commonly, a yarn over is worked among knit stitches on a right-side row. To work the yarn over, bring the yarn in between the needles to the front of the work and then up and over the needle.

There are instances where a yarn over will be worked in the other direction. In this case, bring the yarn up over the needle, from back to front, and then in between the needles to the back. In both cases, the next stitch is worked to lock the yarn over in place.

With Yarn in Front

With Yarn in Back

If a pattern says to slip stitch with yarn in front, keep the yarn to the front of the work as you slip the stitch. Unless otherwise indicated in the pattern, the right side/wrong side of the fabric doesn't matter here—with yarn in front means in front of the work as you are currently looking at it.

If a pattern says to slip stitch with yarn in back, keep the yarn to the back of the work as you slip the stitch. Unless otherwise indicated in the pattern, the right side/wrong side of the fabric doesn't matter here—with yarn in back means in back of the work as you are currently looking at it.

Slip a Stitch Knitwise

1. Insert the right-hand needle into the stitch on the left-hand needle as if you are going to knit the stitch.

2. Do NOT knit the stitch; instead, slide it off the left-hand needle to the right-hand needle.

Slip a Stitch Purlwise

If a pattern tells you to slip a stitch and does not indicate knitwise or purlwise, in general, the stitch is assumed to be slipped purlwise.

1. Insert the right-hand needle into the stitch on the left-hand needle as if you are going to purl the stitch.

2. Do NOT purl the stitch; instead, slide it off the left-hand needle to the right-hand needle.

Cast Ons

When knitting, the first thing you need to do is get some stitches on the needle. The number of ways that you can do this is seemingly endless—there are dozens of options. The decision on which cast on to use will depend greatly on your personal preference and project. Here are some of the most common and popular cast ons for you to use in your knitting journey.

Knitted Cast On 18

Long Tail Cast On 19

Alternating Long Tail Cast On 21

German Twisted Cast On 23

Backward Loop Cast On 26

Cable Cast On 28

Picot Cast On 30

Circular Cast On 32

Provisional Cast On 35

Tubular Cast On 38

Knitted Cast On

This is the first cast on I learned and the one I used exclusively for years. It can be used for anything, but I like it for the start of simple projects like scarves and baby blankets. Once the cast on is complete, usually a right-side row is worked as the next row.

1. Leaving a 4"–6" (10.2–15.2cm) yarn tail, start with a slip knot on the left-hand needle. Insert the right-hand needle into the slip knot as if to knit, yarn over, and pull a loop through.

2. Transfer the new stitch from the right-hand needle to the left-hand needle.

3. Knit into the last stitch on the left-hand needle and transfer the new stitch back to the left-hand needle.

4. Repeat the last step until you have the desired number of stitches on the needle.

Long Tail Cast On

This is one of the most popular cast ons, and I can see why. It makes a clean edge with just the right amount of stretch for most knitting projects. I personally use this cast on for starting the majority of my knitting projects. Once the cast on is complete, usually a wrong-side row is worked as the next row.

1. Leaving a 4"–6" (10.2–15.2cm) yarn tail, estimate the length of yarn tail needed by wrapping the yarn around the needle 10 times. This is approximately the yarn needed for 10 stitches in the Long Tail Cast On.

2. Unravel the yarn off the needle and use that length to estimate the long tail needed. Create a slip knot and place it on the knitting needle.

3. With the knitting needle in your right hand, hold the yarn in your left hand so the long tail is going over your thumb and the working yarn is around your index finger.

4. Maneuver the needle under the leftmost strand of yarn on your thumb and up between the strands of yarn on your thumb.

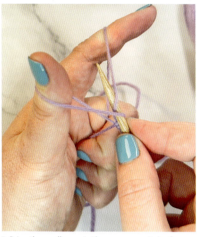

5. Bring the needle over to the yarn on your index finger and "catch" the yarn on the needle.

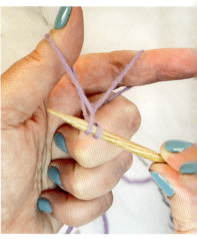

6. Draw the yarn through the loop on your thumb.

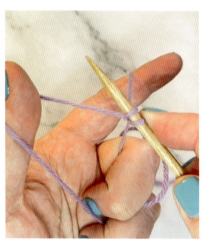

7. Drop the yarn from your thumb and tighten the stitch (but don't overtighten) to the needle.

8. Repeat steps 3–7 until you have the desired number of stitches on the needle.

Alternating Long Tail Cast On

This cast on creates a k1, p1 cast-on edge, perfect for the starts of sweaters and other projects with ribbing patterns.

There are other ways you can use the alternating long tail cast on, including other ribbing patterns and working a two-color alternating long tail cast on. For more information on options for this cast on, follow the QR code to a tutorial.

1. Complete steps 1–3 of Long Tail Cast On (page 19).

2. Maneuver the needle under the rightmost strand of yarn on your index finger, and through the loop on your index finger.

3. Bring the right needle forward and under the rightmost strand of yarn on your thumb.

Cast Ons

4. Move the right needle back down through the loop on your index finger, bringing the strand of yarn from your thumb through the loop to create the stitch. Drop the yarn from your thumb and tighten the stitch (don't overtighten) to the needle. This counts as a purl stitch.

5. Maneuver the needle under the leftmost strand of yarn on your thumb and up between the strands of yarn on your thumb.

6. Bring the needle over to the leftmost strand of yarn on your index finger and "catch" the yarn on the needle, then draw it through the loop on your thumb.

7. Drop the yarn from your thumb and tighten the stitch (don't overtighten) to the needle. This creates a knit stitch.

8. Repeat these steps until you have the desired number of stitches cast on to the needle, ending with step 4 to end on a purl stitch or step 7 to end on a knit stitch.

German Twisted Cast On

This cast on, also known as the Old Norwegian Cast On, is created in a similar manner to the Long Tail Cast On (page 19). The yarn is held in your left hand in the same configuration as the Long Tail Cast On, except you're going under both strands of yarn on your thumb, creating a cast-on edge with a good amount of stretch. This is my favorite cast on for starting cuff-down socks.

1. Leaving a 4"–6" (10.2–15.2cm) yarn tail, estimate the length of yarn tail needed by wrapping the yarn around the needle 15 times. This is approximately the yarn needed for 10 stitches in the German Twisted Cast On.

2. Unravel the yarn off the needle and use that length to create the yarn tail. Create a slip knot and place it on the knitting needle.

3. With the knitting needle in your right hand, hold the yarn in your left hand so that the long tail is going over your thumb and the working yarn is around your index finger.

4. From left to right, maneuver the needle under both strands of yarn on your thumb.

5. Bring the needle over the rightmost strand on your thumb, and down through the loop of yarn on your thumb.

6. Bring the needle over to the yarn on your index finger and "catch" the yarn on the needle.

7. Bend your thumb to "uncross" the loop on your thumb. At this point, the yarn is making an X, and we want to uncross that X.

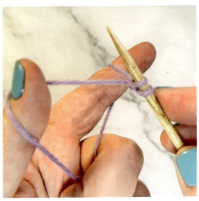

8. Draw the yarn through the loop on your thumb. Drop the yarn from your thumb and tighten the stitch (don't overtighten) to the needle.

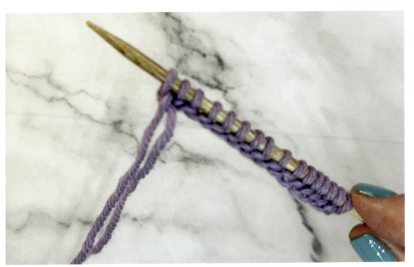

9. Repeat these steps until you have the desired number of stitches cast on to the needle.

Backward Loop Cast On

This is one of the simplest cast ons to execute and is s great one to teach young knitters. Also called the Backward E Cast On or Loop Cast On, this cast on is very stretchy, and it is a great option when you really need a lot of elasticity in your beginning edge.

1. Leaving a 4"–6" (10.2–15.2cm) yarn tail, start with a slip knot on the right-hand needle.

2. With the knitting needle in your right hand, hold the yarn in your left hand so that the working yarn is going over your thumb.

3. Maneuver the needle under the leftmost strand of yarn on your thumb and up between the strands of yarn on your thumb.

4. Drop the yarn from your thumb and tighten the stitch (don't overtighten) to the needle.

5. Repeat these steps until you have the desired number of stitches cast on to the needle.

Cable Cast On

Like the Knitted Cast On (page 18), this cast on is worked by adding knit stitches to the needle on the cast on row. With one slight difference from its counterpart, the cable cast on creates a sturdy, firm cast on, perfect for the underarms of sweaters or anywhere you need a little bit of structure.

1. Leaving a 4"–6" (10.2–15.2cm) yarn tail, start with a slip knot on the left-hand needle. Insert the right-hand needle into the slip knot as if to knit, yarn over, and pull a loop through.

2. Transfer the new stitch from the right-hand needle to the left-hand needle.

3. Insert the needle between the two stitches on the left needle.

4. Yarn over and pull a loop through to create a new stitch. Transfer the new stitch back to the left-hand needle.

5. Repeat the last step until you have the desired number of stitches on the needle.

Cast Ons

Picot Cast On

This fun cast on adds decorative detail to your knitting. I love using this one for baby items! Pair it with the Picot Bind Off (page 50) to finish your project with the same sweet edging. While working with the Picot Cast On, experiment with the number of stitches you cast on and bind off to create a totally different look to your project!

1. Leaving a 4"–6" (10.2–15.2cm) yarn tail, start with a slip knot on the left-hand needle. The slip knot counts as the first stitch. Insert the right-hand needle into the slip knot as if to knit, yarn over, and pull a loop through.

2. Transfer the new stitch from the right-hand needle to the left-hand needle—2 stitches.

3. Using the Cable Cast On (page 28), cast on 2 more stitches—4 stitches.

4. Using the Standard Knitwise Bind Off (page 42), bind off 2 stitches.

5. Slip the stitch purlwise from the right needle to the left needle.

6. Cable Cast On (page 28) 4 stitches.

7. Repeat steps 4–6, ending with step 5, until you have the desired number of stitches on the needle.

Cast Ons

Circular Cast On

The circular cast on is used for starting projects at a center and working outward. Most commonly, you'll see it used on pi shawls, circular tablecloths, and baby blankets, but it can be used for other projects as well. When the cast on is complete, you'll have an odd number of stitches on the needle.

For more information on the circular cast on, follow the QR code to a tutorial.

1. Leaving a 4"–6" (10.2–15.2cm) yarn tail, loop the yarn around two fingers on your left hand, forming an X with the yarn. The yarn tail is crossing under the working yarn. The working yarn is the top leg of the X.

2. Bring the right needle under the right strand and over the left strand on the top half of the X.

3. Bring the tip of the needle down to catch the strand of yarn, and then bring the yarn and needle back under the right strand and into the loop that is formed. This creates the first stitch.

4. Reorient the loop and needle, pinching the loop. Bring the working yarn over your left index finger.

5. Catch the working yarn with the needle. This creates the second stitch.

Cast Ons

6. Insert the needle into the center of the loop and catch the strand of the working yarn.

7. Bring the yarn and needle back through the loop. This creates the next stitch.

8. Repeat steps 4–7, ending with step 7, working into the loop and above the loop until you have the desired number of stitches. This cast on creates an odd number of stitches.

9. Once you start your project and work a few rounds, tug on the tail to pull the hole closed.

Provisional Cast On

The Provisional Cast On is used to create live stitches at the cast-on edge that can be worked later in the project. It is used in interestingly constructed garments and accessories. For this cast on, you'll need smooth, contrasting-colored waste yarn of the same weight, a crochet hook one or two sizes larger than the knitting needle you use for the project, and a locking stitch marker.

1. With contrasting waste yarn, place a slip knot onto the crochet hook.

2. Yarn over and pull the strand of yarn through the loop on the crochet hook to create one chain.

3. Repeat step 2 until you have a few more crochet chains than the number of stitches you need for your project. For this sample, I crocheted a chain of 20 stitches for casting on 16 stitches.

4. Cut the waste yarn and pull the end through the last loop to secure it. Use a locking stitch marker to mark this end of the chain.

5. The front of the chain looks like a braid. Turn the chain over to the back, where there are "bumps." This is where stitches will be picked up with the knitting needle. Insert the right needle into the back bump of the first chain.

6. With the working yarn, yarn over and pull a stitch through—1 stitch cast on.

7. Repeat steps 5 and 6, working into the next crochet chain across until you have the desired number of stitches.

8. Remember, you will have a few extra crochet chains. This completes the cast on and your first row of knitting. For most patterns the next row will be a wrong-side row.

9. To work the live stitches from the provisional cast-on edge, undo the crochet chain from the side of the chain with the locking stitch marker.

10. Carefully unravel the crochet chain, slipping the live stitches on the knitting needle.

11. Repeat until all the stitches are on the knitting needle. Enjoy knitting in the opposite direction!

Cast Ons 37

Tubular Cast On

The Tubular Cast On creates a smooth, finished edge perfect for ribbing patterns, as demonstrated here in a 1x1 (knit 1 stitch, purl 1 stitch) rib pattern. It can be worked in various configurations, making it perfect for projects like socks and hats.

1. Using contrasting waste yarn, cast on half the number of stitches needed for your project, using the Long Tail Cast On (page 19) or the cast on method of your choice.

2. Continuing with waste yarn, work 3 or 4 rows of Stockinette stitch (knit on right side/purl on wrong side) with waste yarn, ending on a right-side row.

3. On the next wrong-side row, switch to your main yarn—the yarn you want to use for the project—and work 4 rows in Stockinette stitch, ending on a right-side row.

4. Next row (wrong side), purl 1 stitch.

5. With the right needle, pick up the first purl bump of the main yarn 4 rows below.

6. Place the stitch on your left needle and knit the stitch.

7. Purl 1 stitch.

8. Repeat steps 5–7, ending with step 7, until all stitches have been worked.

9. Work several rows of the 1x1 rib pattern, then cut the waste yarn and remove it from the project.

Bind Offs

When your knitting is done, it's time to bind off. Just like the cast ons, there's no shortage of ways to bind off (also called "cast off" in some regions of the world). Let's explore a variety of bind offs, from basic to decorative and everything in between.

Standard Knitwise Bind Off 42

Knit Two Stitches Together Through the Back Loop Bind Off.....44

Bind Off in Pattern 46

Elastic Bind Off 48

Picot Bind Off.....................50

Cable Bind Off 52

I-Cord Bind Off 54

Three-Needle Bind Off 56

Grafting.........................58

Tubular Bind Off 61

Standard Knitwise Bind Off

This is typically the first bind off one learns when starting your knitting journey. It's easy, it's simple, and it's the perfect bind off for most knitting projects.

1. Knit the first 2 stitches independently—2 stitches on the right-hand needle.

2. From the front, insert the left-hand needle into the first stitch that was knit. Pass the first stitch over the second stitch and off of the needle—1 stitch on the right-hand needle.

3. Knit the next stitch—2 stitches on the right-hand needle.

4. Repeat steps 2 and 3 until 1 stitch remains on the right-hand needle.

5. Trim the yarn, leaving 4"–6" (10.2–15.2cm) of tail to weave in later. Draw the yarn through the last loop to fasten it off.

NOTE

This bind off can be worked purlwise as well. Purl the stitches across the row while working the bind off.

Knit Two Stitches Together Through the Back Loop Bind Off

The Knit Two Stitches Together Through the Back Loop (k2tog tbl) Bind Off is my favorite bind off for knitting shawls or other projects where I need a stretchy, loose bind-off edge. If you tend to bind off tightly, try using a needle one or two sizes larger as well.

1. Knit the first 2 stitches together through the back loops.

2. Slip the stitch purlwise from the right needle to the left needle.

3. Knit 2 together through the back loops.

4. Repeat steps 2 and 3 until 1 stitch remains on the right-hand needle.

5. Trim the yarn, leaving 4"–6" (10.2–15.2cm) of tail to weave in later. Draw the yarn through the last loop to fasten it off.

Bind Offs

Bind Off in Pattern

Binding off in pattern means you'll be working the stitches as they appear on the needle (knit the knit stitches and purl the purl stitches). In the example, I'm working a 1x1 (k1, p1) ribbing pattern. But you can work this bind off in a variety of configurations. It is used for projects that end in a ribbing pattern, like sweaters and toe-up socks. Try it on your next project with ribbing!

1. Knit the knit stitch, purl the purl stitch—2 stitches on the right needle.

2. From the front, insert the left-hand needle into the first stitch that was worked.

3. Pass the first stitch over the second stitch and off the needle—1 stitch on the right-hand needle.

4. Work the next stitch as it appears (knit the knit stitch or purl the purl stitch)—2 stitches on the right-hand needle.

5. Repeat steps 2–4 until 1 stitch remains on the right-hand needle.

6. Trim the yarn, leaving 4"–6" (10.2–15.2cm) of tail to weave in later. Draw the yarn through the last loop to fasten it off.

NOTE

An example of binding off in a 2x2 (k2, p2) ribbing pattern.

Bind Offs 47

Elastic Bind Off

The elastic bind off is another favorite for my shawl knitters. This bind off creates a very stretchy final edge, making it perfect for top-down shawls.

1. Knit 2 stitches.

2. Bring the left needle through the front of the 2 stitches on the right needle.

3. Knit the 2 stitches together through their back loops (k2tog tbl).

4. Knit 1 stitch—2 stitches on the right needle.

5. Repeat steps 2–4 until 1 stitch remains on the right needle.

6. Trim the yarn, leaving 4"–6" (10.2–15.2cm) of tail to weave in later. Draw the yarn through the last loop to fasten it off.

Picot Bind Off

The Picot Bind Off is a decorative bind off that goes perfectly with the Picot Cast On (page 30). Like the cast on, I love adding this one to baby items. It also adds a lovely detail to a shawl.

1. Cable Cast On (page 28) 2 stitches.

2. Bind off 4 stitches using the Knitwise Bind Off (page 42)—1 stitch remains on the right needle.

3. Slip the stitch purlwise from the right needle to the left needle.

4. Repeat steps 1–3 until all the stitches have been worked.

5. Trim the yarn, leaving 4"–6" (10.2–15.2cm) of tail to weave in later. Draw the yarn through the last loop to fasten it off.

Cable Bind Off

The Cable Bind Off is designed to be paired with the Cable Cast On (page 28). It's a standard bind off, with a literal twist—the stitches are being twisted while binding off to create a firm edge. This might be a good choice for a structured project, like the shoulder of a sweater.

1. Knit 2 stitches.

2. Pass the first stitch over the second stitch—1 stitch remains on the right needle.

3. Slip the stitch from the right needle to the left needle through the front loop, creating a twist.

4. Slip the stitch back to the right needle through the back loop, creating another twist.

5. Knit 1 stitch—2 stitches are on the right needle.

6. Repeat steps 2–5 until all the stitches have been bound off and 1 stitch remains.

7. Trim the yarn, leaving 4"–6" (10.2–15.2cm) of tail to weave in later. Draw the yarn through the last loop to fasten it off.

I-Cord Bind Off

The I-Cord Bind Off is another decorative bind off that adds interest and flexibility onto the edge of your project. You can add it to many different projects, though it's another favorite of mine to work into a shawl.

1. With the right side facing, and using the Knitted Cast On (page 18), cast on 3 stitches.

2. Knit 2 stitches.

3. Knit 2 stitches together through the back loops (k2tog tbl).

4. Slip the 3 stitches purlwise from the right needle to the left needle.

5. Repeat steps 2–4 until all the stitches have been bound off and the 3 stitches of the I-cord remain.

6. Bind off the last 3 stitches using a Standard Knitwise Bind Off (page 42).

7. Trim the yarn, leaving 4"–6" (10.2–15.2cm) of tail to weave in later. Draw the yarn through the last loop to fasten it off.

Three-Needle Bind Off

The Three-Needle Bind Off creates a seam in your knitting, which can be useful for projects like sweaters. Like many of these bind offs, it can be worked in a variety of configurations to create the look you want for your project. To do this project, you'll need an extra knitting needle the same size as the primary needle you're using.

1. Place 2 pieces of knitted fabric wrong sides together as the left needles. Make sure to have the same number of stitches on each needle.

2. Use a third needle to go through the first stitch on both needles in your left hand, and knit them together as 1 stitch—1 stitch on the right needle.

3. Work the next stitch by going through the first stitch on both needles in your left hand, and knit them together as 1 stitch—2 stitches on the right needle.

4. Using the back-left needle, pass the first stitch on the right needle over the second stitch—1 stitch remains on the right needle.

5. Repeat steps 3 and 4 until all the stitches have been bound off and 1 stitch remains.

6. Trim the yarn, leaving 4"–6" (10.2–15.2cm) of tail to weave in later. Draw the yarn through the last loop to fasten it off.

Grafting

Grafting, also called the Kitchener stitch, is a method of finishing your knitting by working live stitches together seamlessly, commonly used to finish the toes of socks. You'll need a tapestry or yarn needle.

1. Place 2 pieces of knitted fabric wrong sides together. Make sure to have the same number of stitches on each needle.

2. Using a length of yarn three to four times the width of the piece to be grafted together, thread the yarn onto the tapestry needle. I'm using a contrasting color here, but in most cases, you will use the working yarn from your project to graft the stitches.

3. Bring the tapestry needle through the first stitch on the front needle as if to purl. Do not remove the stitch from the knitting needle.

4. Bring the tapestry needle through the first stitch on the back needle as if to knit. Do not remove the stitch from the knitting needle.

5. Bring the tapestry needle through the first stitch on the front needle as if to knit, and remove the stitch from the knitting needle.

6. Bring the tapestry needle through the next stitch on the front needle as if to purl, and leave it on the knitting needle.

Bind Offs 59

7. Bring the tapestry through the first stitch on the back needle as if to purl, and remove the stitch from the knitting needle.

8. Bring the tapestry needle through the next stitch on the back needle as if to knit, and leave it on the knitting needle.

9. Repeat steps 5–8 until 1 stitch remains on each needle.

10. Bring the tapestry needle through the stitch on the front needle as if to knit, and remove it. Bring the tapestry needle through the stitch on the back needle as if to purl and remove it. Once the grafting is complete, trim the yarn, leaving 4"–6" (10.2–15.2cm) of tail to weave in later. If necessary, use the tip of the tapestry or knitting needle to tighten up the grafted stitches as desired.

Tubular Bind Off

The Tubular Bind Off is a method of finishing your final edge of knitting with a truly polished look, great for scarves and sweaters. Use it in conjunction with the Tubular Cast On (page 38) for very neat edges on your project. Like its cast-on counterpart, this bind off can be set up in different configurations. Here, it is demonstrated in 1x1 (K1, P1) ribbing over an odd number of stitches. You'll need two spare knitting needles the same size as the primary needle you are using, as well as a tapestry or yarn needle.

1. Work the project 2 rows less than the desired final length, ending on a wrong-side row.

2. On the next right-side row, knit 1 stitch, slip the next purl stitch with yarn in front, and repeat across, ending with 1 knit stitch.

3. Repeat step 2, working in the established pattern (knit the knit stitches, slip 1 stitch purlwise with yarn in front for purl stitches) for another 3 rows—4 rows worked total.

4. Using two spare needles and slipping all stitches purlwise, slip the knit stitches to the front needle, and the purl stitches to the back needle, working across the row until all the stitches are separated on the two needles.

5. Using a tapestry or yarn needle, graft the stitches together (see page 58). Once the grafting is complete, trim the yarn, leaving 4"–6" (10.2–15.2cm) of tail to weave in later.

NOTE

When worked over an odd number of stitches, one needle will have 1 more stitch than the other. Work across the row, working 2 stitches as 1 when you come to the final stitches on the needle.

Index

abbreviations (knitting), 11
alternating long tail cast on, 21

backward E cast on, 26
backward loop cast on, 26
bind off: cable, 52; elastic, 48; grafting, 58; I-cord, 54; Kitchener stitch, 58; knit two stitches together through the back loop, 44; picot, 50; standard knitwise, 42; three needle, 56; tubular, 61
bind off in pattern, 46
bind offs, choosing, 11
bulky yarn, 8

cable bind off, 52
cable cast on, 28
cast on: alternating long tail, 21; backward E, 26; backward loop, 26; cable, 28; circular, 32; German twisted, 23; knitted, 18; long tail, 19; loop, 26; old Norwegian, 23; picot, 30; provisional, 35; tubular, 38
cast ons, choosing, 11
circular cast on, 32
circular needles, 6
crochet hook, 10

double-pointed needles (DPNs), 6

elastic bind off, 48
English method of knitting, 5

fingering yarn, 8

gauge, 8
German twisted cast on, 23
grafting, 58

I-cord bind off, 54

Kitchener stitch, 58
knit stitch, 13
knit two stitches together through back loop bind off, 44
knitted cast on, 18
knitting needles, 6; circular, 6; double-pointed, 6; sizes, 7; straight, 6

long tail cast on, 19
loop cast on, 26

measuring tape, 10

needles (knitting): circular, 6; double-pointed, 6; sizes, 7; straight, 6
needles, tapestry, 10
notions, 10

old Norwegian cast on, 23

picot bind off, 50
picot cast on, 30
provisional cast on, 35
purl stitch, 14

scissors, 10
slip a stitch: knitwise, 16; purlwise, 16
slip knot, 12
snips, 10
standard knitwise bind off, 42
stitch markers, 10
stitch: knit, 13; purl, 14; slip a, knitwise, 16; slip a, purlwise, 16
straight needles, 6

tapestry needles, 10
three-needle bind off, 56
throwing method of knitting, 5
tubular bind off, 61
tubular cast on, 38

with yarn in back, 15
with yarn in front, 15
working yarn, 11
worsted yarn, 8

yarn over, 15
yarn weight guide, 9
yarn, 8: bulky, 8; fingering, 8; in back, 15; in front, 15; working, 11; worsted, 8

About the Author

Jen Lucas has been knitting for over two decades. She has designed hundreds of knitting and crochet patterns for yarn companies, magazines, and books, in addition to her dozens of self-published designs. Jen is the author of several knitting books, including the best seller *Sock-Yarn Shawls.* She lives in Northern Illinois with her husband, Alex, and a home full of crafts. Learn more about Jen at *craftyjencrafts.com.*

OTHER TITLES BY JEN LUCAS:

Pocket Guide to Crochet
Pocket Guide to Knitting
Big Book of Knitted Shawls